Phillips, Craig & Dean

LET THE WORSHIPPERS ARISE

Piano · Vocal · Guitar

ISBN 0-634-08943-9

HAL·LEONARD®
CORPORATION
7777 W. BLUEMOUND RD. P.O. BOX 13819 MILWAUKEE, WI 53213

Visit Hal Leonard Online at
www.halleonard.com

Phillips, Craig & Dean

LET THE WORSHIPPERS ARISE

FRIEND OF GOD

Words and Music by MICHAEL GUNGOR
and ISRAEL HOUGHTON

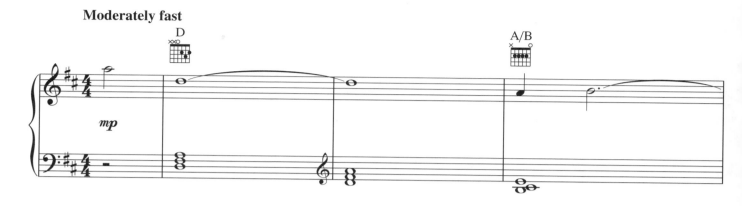

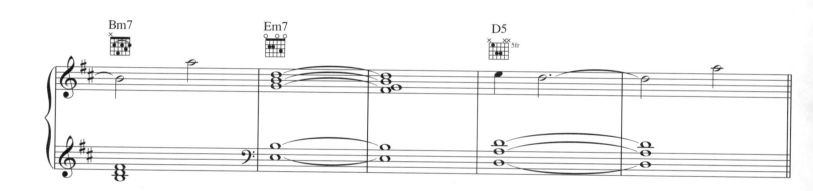

Who am I ___ that You ___ are mind-ful ___ of ___ me,

BECAUSE I'M FORGIVEN

Words and Music by SHAWN CRAIG,
MARC JUDD and SCOTT REED

Moderately fast

it's be - cause ___ I'm ___ for - giv -

- en. ___

G/D

D

It's be - cause ___ I ___ am free. ___

I'm _____ free. _____

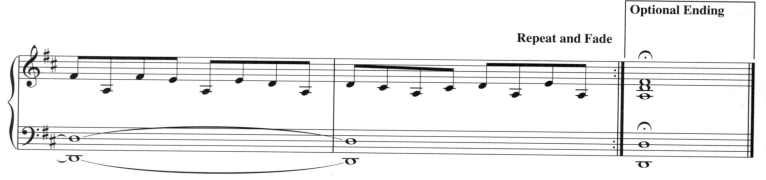

Repeat and Fade

Optional Ending

YOU ARE GOD ALONE
(not a god)

Words and Music by BILLY J. FOOTE
and CINDY FOOTE

You are not a god cre - at - ed by hu - man hands.

*Recorded a half step lower.

24

un - stop - pa - ble, ___ that's what You are. ___

Optional Ending

Repeat and Fade

IN CHRIST ALONE
(medley)

Words and Music by KEITH GETTY
and STUART TOWNEND

IN CHRIST ALONE
Words and Music by DON KOCH
and SHAWN CRAIG

LET THE WORSHIPPERS ARISE

Words and Music by
MICHAEL FERRIN

Recorded a half step lower.

MY REDEEMER LIVES

Words and Music by
REUBEN MORGAN

*Recorded a half step lower.

BE THE PRAISE OF MY HEART

Words and Music by DAN DEAN
and GARY SADLER

AWAKE MY SOUL
(Christ Is Formed In Me)

Words and Music by
RANDY PHILLIPS

I'M MAKING MELODY

Words and Music by
MATT REDMAN

Moderately fast Rock

I'm mak-ing mel-o-dy

in my heart to You.

I'm mak-ing mel-o-dy

in my heart to You.

Pour - ing out Your praise

MIGHTY IS THE POWER
OF THE CROSS

Words and Music by SHAWN CRAIG
and CHRIS TOMLIN

In a slow two

Lyrics:
What can take ___ a dy-ing man ___ and raise him up ___ to life ___ a - gain?

What can heal ___ the wound - ed soul, ___ what can make ___ us white ___

Recorded a half step lower.

WONDERFUL, MERCIFUL SAVIOR

Words and Music by DAWN RODGERS
and ERIC WYSE

Wonderful, merciful Savior, precious Redeemer and Friend.

MORE OF THE BEST PRAISE & WORSHIP SONGBOOKS

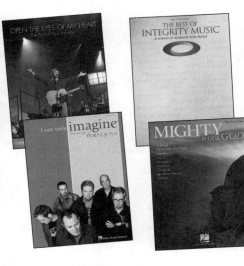

OPEN THE EYES OF MY HEART
The Best of Paul Baloche

Paul Baloche describes his music career as "journaling his process of his walk with the Lord." This songbook features 12 of his best praise & worship favorites: Above All • All the Earth Will Sing Your Praises • Arise • Celebrate the Lord of Love • I Love to Be in Your Presence • I See the Lord • Offering • Open the Eyes of My Heart • Praise Adonai • Revival Fire Fall • Rise Up and Praise Him • Sing Out.

_____08739746 Piano/Vocal/Guitar $14.95

THE BEST OF INTEGRITY MUSIC
25 Songs of Worship and Praise

More than two dozen of the best P&W songs from Integrity: Above All • Ancient of Days • Celebrate Jesus • Firm Foundation • Give Thanks • Mighty Is Our God • Open the Eyes of My Heart • This Is the Day • Trading My Sorrows • You Are Good • and more.

_____08739790 Piano/Vocal/Guitar $16.95

THE BEST OF MODERN WORSHIP

15 of today's wonderful sacred songs: Cannot Say Enough • Everyday • Fields of Grace • Freedom • Friend of God • God Is Great • Here I Am to Worship • I Can Only Imagine • Lord, You Have My Heart • Meet with Me • Open the Eyes of My Heart • Sing for Joy • Trading My Sorrows • Word of God Speak • You Are My King (Amazing Love).

_____08739747 Piano/Vocal/Guitar $14.95

GIVE THANKS – THE BEST OF HOSANNA! MUSIC
25 Worship Favorites

This superb best-of collection features 25 worship favorites published by Hosanna! Music: Ancient of Days • Celebrate Jesus • I Worship You, Almighty God • More Precious Than Silver • My Redeemer Lives • Shout to the Lord • and more.

_____08739729 Piano/Vocal/Guitar..................$14.95
_____08739745 Easy Piano.............................$12.95

THE BEST OF HILLSONG

25 of the most popular songs from Hillsong artists and writers, including: All Things Are Possible • Awesome in This Place • Blessed • Eagle's Wings • God Is Great • Holy Spirit Rain Down • I Give You My Heart • Jesus, What a Beautiful Name • The Potter's Hand • Shout to the Lord • Worthy Is the Lamb • You Are Near • and more.

_____08739789 Piano/Vocal/Guitar $16.95

¡WORSH!P CHRISTMAS
A Total Christmas Worship Experience

Selections from the popular Christmas album, including: Away in a Manger • The Birthday of a King • Breath of Heaven (Mary's Song) • Come, Thou Long-Expected Jesus • Hallelujah • Joy to the World/Heaven and Nature Sing • One Small Child/More Precious Than Silver • What Child Is This? • You Are Emmanuel/Emmanuel • and more.

_____08739788 Piano/Vocal/Guitar $16.95

I CAN ONLY IMAGINE – THE SONGS OF MERCYME

10 of the most recognizable songs from this popular Contemporary Christian group, including the smash hit "I Can Only Imagine," plus: Cannot Say Enough • Here with Me • Homesick • How Great Is Your Love • The Love of God • Spoken For • Unaware • Where You Lead Me • Word of God Speak.

_____08739803 Piano Solo.............................$12.95

MIGHTY IS OUR GOD
25 Songs of Worship and Praise

Piano/Vocal/Guitar arrangements of more than two dozen beloved P&W songs, including: Above All • Firm Foundation • I Stand in Awe • Lord Most High • Open the Eyes of My Heart • Sing for Joy • Think About His Love • and more.

_____08739744 Piano/Vocal/Guitar $14.95

Prices & contents subject to change without notice.

FOR MORE INFORMATION,
SEE YOUR LOCAL MUSIC DEALER,
OR WRITE TO:

HAL•LEONARD®
CORPORATION
7777 W. BLUEMOUND RD. P.O. BOX 13819
MILWAUKEE, WISCONSIN 53213
www.halleonard.com

GOD WILL MAKE A WAY: THE BEST OF DON MOEN

We're very proud to present this matching songbook featuring 19 greatest hits from this Dove Award-winning singer/songwriter. Includes: Celebrate Jesus • Give Thanks • God Will Make a Way • God with Us Medley • Heal Me O Lord • Here We Are • I Offer My Life • I Will Sing • Let Your Glory Fall • Shout to the Lord • We Give You Glory • You Make Me Lie Down in Green Pastures • Your Steadfast Love • and more.

_____08739297 Piano/Vocal/Guitar $16.95

PHILLIPS, CRAIG & DEAN – LET THE WORSHIPPERS ARISE

Matching folio to the newest release from this trio of pastors. Songs include: Friend of God • Because I'm Forgiven • You Are God Alone (not a god) • In Christ Alone (Medley) • Let the Worshippers Arise • My Redeemer Lives • Be the Praise of My Heart • Awake My Soul (Christ Is Formed in Me) • Making Melody • Mighty Is the Power of the Cross • Wonderful Merciful Savior.

_____08739804 Piano/Vocal/Guitar..................$16.95

DEREK WEBB – SHE MUST AND SHALL GO FREE

CCM magazine has called Derek Webb, a former member of the popular folk-rock group Caedmon's Call, "one of the 25 most important artists shaping Christian music today." His first solo release, this album immediately produced two hit singles: the title track and "Take to the World." Our matching folio contains those songs and 9 more: Awake My Soul • Beloved • The Church • Crooked Deep Down • Lover • Nobody Loves Me • Nothing (Without You) • Saint and Sinner • Wedding Dress.

_____08739730 Piano/Vocal/Guitar $14.95

COME INTO HIS PRESENCE
Songs of Worship for Solo Piano

Features 12 beautiful piano solo arrangements of worship favorites: Above All • Blessed Be the Lord God Almighty • Breathe • Come Into His Presence • Draw Me Close • Give Thanks • God Will Make a Way • Jesus, Name Above All Names/Blessed Be the Name of the Lord • Lord Have Mercy • More Precious Than Silver • Open the Eyes of My Heart • Shout to the Lord.

_____08739299 Piano Solo.............................$12.95